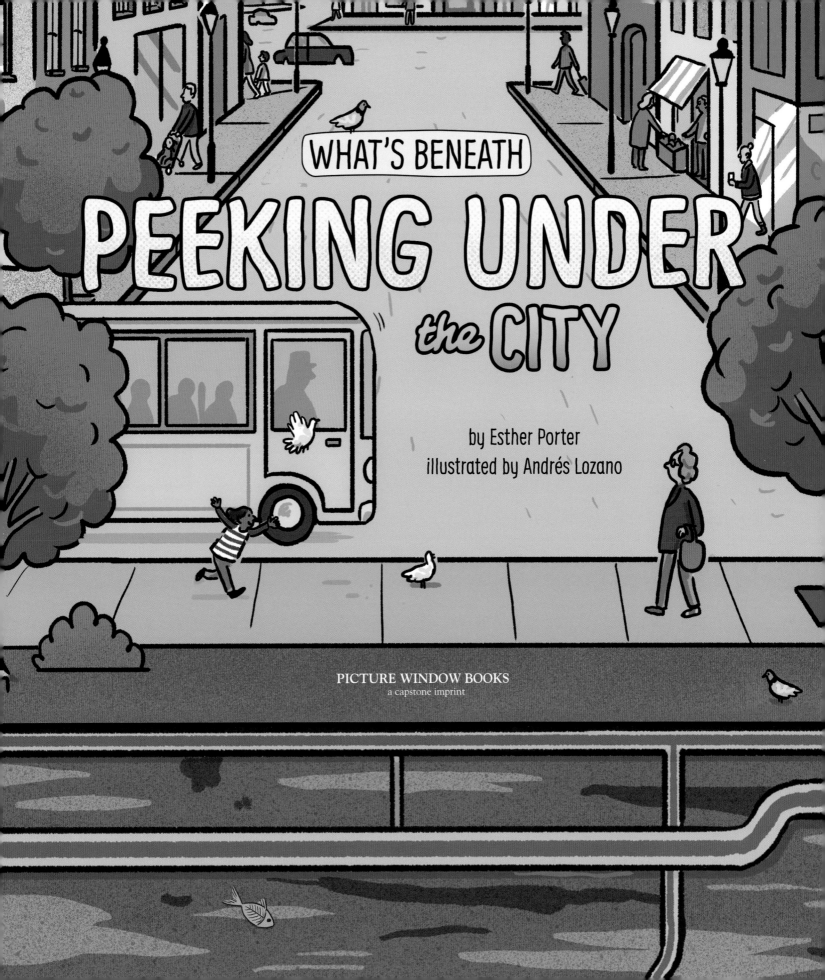

WHAT'S BENEATH

PEEKING UNDER the CITY

by Esther Porter

illustrated by Andrés Lozano

PICTURE WINDOW BOOKS
a capstone imprint

Welcome to the big city!
Do you see the tall buildings and bright lights?
See the people hurrying up and down the streets?
Hear the music, sirens, and car horns?

So much happens in a city ABOVE ground. What happens BELOW?
Flip the page to peek beneath ...

Beneath a city lie the systems that make people's lives easier. Tubes called conduits carry cables. Pipes bring in clean water and take out dirty water. Other pipes bring in gas or steam for power. Tunnels allow people to move from place to place.

All of these systems are carefully planned. Civil engineers do the planning. They work closely with builders to decide where everything needs to go.

Power Up!

What are all these lines? Thousands of miles of cables! Most cables run underground. Burying cables keeps them safe from wind, rain, and ice. Some cables carry power to homes and businesses. Others carry information for computers and TVs.

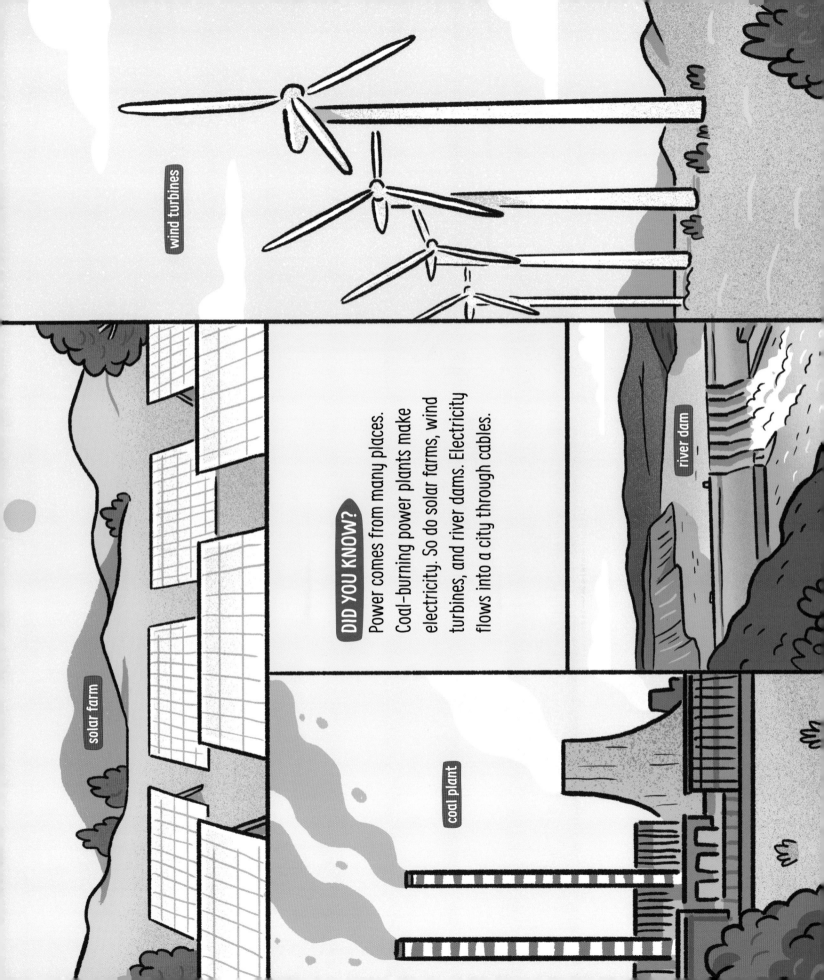

wind turbines

solar farm

river dam

coal plant

DID YOU KNOW?

Power comes from many places. Coal-burning power plants make electricity. So do solar farms, wind turbines, and river dams. Electricity flows into a city through cables.

Thirsty?

People need clean water for drinking, washing, and cooking. Where does it come from?

Water comes from lakes, rivers, and reservoirs. It's cleaned in water treatment plants. Then it's piped into a city. Water flows first through large pipes called mains. Smaller pipes called submains carry water from the mains to branch lines. Branch lines carry water into buildings. In large cities more than 1 billion gallons (3.8 billion liters) of water may flow every day.

DID YOU KNOW?

New York City sits over underground streams. People covered the streams with dirt to make room for new buildings. Hundreds of years ago, people traveled through the city by canoe.

Hot and Cold

Many underground pipes carry water. But this maze of pipes carries natural gas. Natural gas heats buildings in winter. During summer it cools them.

Natural gas can travel thousands of miles from a power plant to a city. See how the pipes get smaller near homes and businesses? The smaller pipes squeeze the gas and keep it moving.

DID YOU KNOW?

Natural gas is a fossil fuel. People mine for natural gas by drilling deep into the earth. Then power plants purify the gas and send it out to cities.

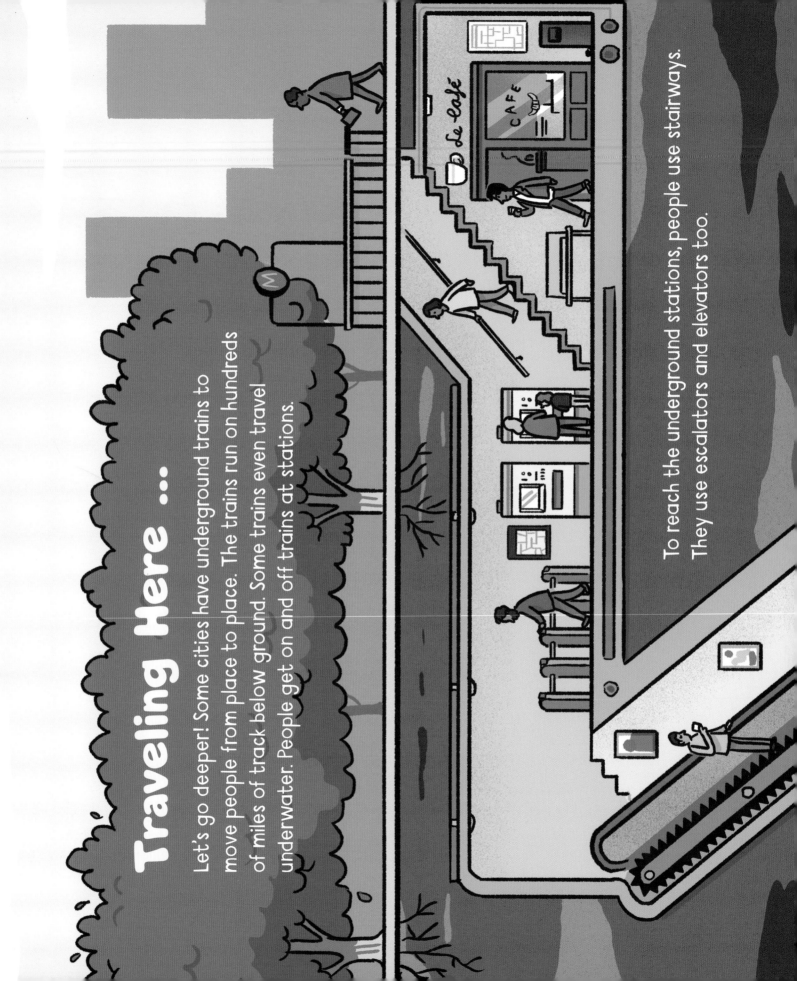

Traveling Here ...

Let's go deeper! Some cities have underground trains to move people from place to place. The trains run on hundreds of miles of track below ground. Some trains even travel underwater. People get on and off trains at stations.

To reach the underground stations, people use stairways. They use escalators and elevators too.

station

escalator

DID YOU KNOW?

Tokyo, Japan, has the world's busiest underground train system. About 8.7 million people ride Tokyo Metro every day.

And Traveling There ...

Not all underground tunnels have subway tracks. Some tunnels hold roadways. Putting roads underground leaves more space above ground for people to live.

Beneath Boston, Massachusetts, cars zoom on highways 8 to 10 lanes wide. To dig tunnels that deep and wide, workers moved a lot of dirt. They filled more than 541,000 trucks!

Dino-rific!

Fossils are the remains of plants or animals from long ago. The remains sank deep into the earth. Over thousands of years, they hardened into rock. Today when workers dig below cities, they often find fossils.

Sometimes the fossils are dinosaur bones. Builders in China once found **43** fossilized dinosaur eggs at their work site.

How many eggs can you find here?

When people die they are often buried underground. See the room beneath the church? It's called a crypt. Crypts are used as burial spaces. Old churches often have underground crypts.

catacomb

Long ago, people in Europe buried their dead in catacombs. Catacombs can have many miles of caves and tunnels. Below Paris, France, lie catacombs. They hold the bones of more than 6 million people.

Standing Tall

foundations

How do big, tall buildings keep from falling over? Like giant trees they need strong roots! A building's foundation is like a tree's roots. People set foundations for the tallest city buildings into solid bedrock. See how deep the foundations reach? They go far, far beneath the city.

Good-bye, Water

Clean water is necessary in our lives. So is getting rid of dirty water. Pipes carry waste from buildings to wastewater treatment plants. Plant workers clean the water. Then they send it back to lakes and rivers.

Rain collects in city storm drains. From drains, water flows through pipes or waterways called aqueducts. Storm drain water is not cleaned. It runs right into nearby bodies of water.

DID YOU KNOW?
An alligator was spotted in the New York City sewer system in 1935. No one knows how it got there. None have been seen since.

Water Supply

What do you find hundreds of feet below street level? **MORE** water!

It's important for a city to have lots of water. It's **VERY** important for cities with millions of people. A special water tunnel will one day stretch 60 miles (97 kilometers) through New York City. It will carry 1.3 billion gallons (4.9 billion liters) of water per day.

From Long Ago

You can find all sorts of things buried under a city. Bones, shells, and fossils?

Of course!

You can find cannonballs, anchors, and whole ships. Metal pipes, pottery, and glass bottles might be there too. You might even find an entire ancient city! Scientists study the things they dig up. They use them to find out how people lived in the past. It's like exploring an underground museum.

How about full skeletons? Yes!

Coins and dishes? Sure!

Back on the street, cars honk, lights flash, and people rush home for dinner. A city is a busy place above ground.

GLOSSARY

ancient—from a long time ago

aqueduct—a large channel built to carry water

bedrock—a layer of solid rock beneath the layers of soil and loose gravel broken up by weathering

catacomb—an underground network of burial tunnels and chambers

civil engineer—a person who works on the design, construction, or maintenance of any structure

conduit—a protective tube that contains wires and cables

crypt—a burial chamber

escalator—a moving staircase

fossil—the remains or traces of an animal or a plant, preserved as rock

fossil fuel—a natural fuel formed from the remains of plants and animals; coal, oil, and natural gas are fossil fuels

purify—to make something clean

reservoir—a holding area for large amounts of water

sewer—an underground system of drains and pipes that carries dirty water

solar—having to do with the sun

turbine—an engine powered by steam, water, wind, or gas passing across the blades of a fanlike device and making it spin

CRITICAL THINKING USING THE COMMON CORE

1. Why do you think power and information cables lie close to the surface and not deep underground? (Integration of Knowledge and Ideas)

2. Explain how drinking water gets to a building in a city. (Key Ideas and Details)

3. What do civil engineers do? And why are they important? (Integration of Knowledge and Ideas)

READ MORE

Lassieur, Allison. *Subways in Action*. Transportation Zone. Mankato, Minn.: Capstone Press, 2012.

Niemann, Christoph. *Subway*. New York: Greenwillow Books, 2010.

Spiegelman, Nadja. *Lost in NYC: A Subway Adventure*. New York: TOON Books, 2015.

I T RN T SIT

FactHound offers a safe, fun way to find Internet sites related to this book. All of the sites on FactHound have been researched by our staff.

Here's all you do:

Visit www.facthound.com

Type in this code: 9781479586653

Super-cool stuff! Check out projects, games and lots more at **www.capstonekids.com**

Special thanks to our adviser, Erin Santini Bell, PhD, PE, Civil Engineering, University of New Hampshire, for her expertise.

Picture Window Books are published by Capstone,
1710 Roe Crest Drive, North Mankato, Minnesota 56003
www.mycapstone.com

Library of Congress Cataloging-in-Publication Data
Cataloging-in-publication information is on file with the Library of Congress.
ISBN 978-1-4795-8665-3 (library binding)
ISBN 978-1-4795-8669-1 (paperback)
ISBN 978-1-4795-8673-8 (eBook PDF)

Editor: Jill Kalz
Designer: Russell Griesmer
Creative Director: Nathan Gassman
Production Specialist: Katy LaVigne
The illustrations in this book were created digitally.

Printed and bound in US
007536CGS16

LOOK FOR ALL THE BOOKS IN THE SERIES:

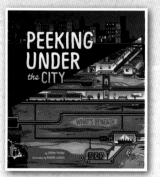
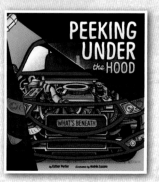